Wandering Bone

Meadowlark (an imprint of Chasing Tigers Press)
meadowlark-books.com
P.O. Box 333, Emporia, KS 66801

Copyright © 2017 Olive Sullivan

All rights reserved. This book or any portion thereof
may not be reproduced or used in any manner whatsoever
without the express written permission of the author
except for the use of brief quotations in a book review.

Cover art by Angie Pickman, Rural Pearl Studio, www.ruralpearl.com

ISBN: 978-0-9966801-8-9

Library of Congress Control Number: 2017915549

Wandering Bone

Poems by Olive L. Sullivan

A MEADOWLARK BOOK

to my parents, Mary-Kate and Victor Sullivan,
my earliest and most enduring traveling companions

"You pass through places
and places pass through you.
You carry them with you
on the soles of your travelin' shoes."

— "The Littlest Birds,"
  by The Be Good Tanyas

Contents

Everlasting Blue

The Universe Begins . . . 3
The Blue Inside . . . 4
As Darkness Falls . . . 5
Fool's Gold . . . 7
The Things We Know . . . 8
Family Bed . . . 10
Family Photos . . . 11
Blue . . . 13
On the Dublin-Liverpool Ferry . . . 15
November Falling . . . 16
The Black Dog . . . 17
Baghdad . . . 20
Requiem on a November Night . . . 21
Oblivion Tango . . . 23
Wandering Bone . . . 24
Think Stars, Count Sheep . . . 25
Divorcing . . . 26
Landslip . . . 27
Green How I Want You . . . 28
Winter Down . . . 29

The Edge of the Map

Half a World Away . . . 33
The Black Dog Follows . . . 34
La Lupa . . . 35
Avebury . . . 36

The Galapagos Blue-Foot Strut . . . 37
Barqerizo Moreño . . . 38
Weekend Away . . . 39
The Wisdom of the Staircase . . . 41
The Edge of the Map . . . 42
Tortugero . . . 43
What the Mosquito Said . . . 44
June 12 in Paraguay . . . 46
Barrio San Jeronimo . . . 49
Ghost City . . . 51
The Heart of Giocalto . . . 52
The Bone Goddess . . . 54
Carrying Darkness . . . 55
Foreign Places . . . 56
Pilgrimage . . . 57
Election Year . . . 59
The Angel of Nagasaki . . . 61
The Bulls of Marroquin . . . 63
Spain Wins the World Cup, 2010 . . . 64
Souvenir . . . 65
The Seventh Year . . . 66
Sunset on Lake Michigan . . . 67
Driving West . . . 68
Coming Back from New Mexico at Night . . . 69
Fountain of Desire . . . 70
Gas Station Guru . . . 71

Everyday Mermaids

Homecoming . . . 75
Girl, Recovering . . . 76
Rasp . . . 77

Going to La Gruta After
      You Leave for Kansas . . . 78
Kiosk . . . 79
Smiley's Bar . . . 80
Elephant Jam . . . 81
Salsa Mezcla . . . 83
Pin Oak . . . 84
Praise Song for the River . . . 85
Lake Pend Oreille . . . 86
Labyrinth . . . 87
Still . . . 88
Tallgrass . . . 89
Kitchen Ballet . . . 90
Everyday Mermaids . . . 91
Bless This House . . . 92

About the Poet . . . 94
Acknowledgments . . . 95
Credits . . . 97

Everlasting Blue

The Universe Begins

The universe begins and
two golden grosbeaks pop into being
against a cerulean sky.
God laughs with pleasure.
She snaps her fingers and
a single pronghorn antelope
lifts his head from the high plains
munching a mouthful of sage.
Six bighorn sheep move up the mountainside
and a coyote lopes through a meadow of buttercups.
A beaver swims upstream
to pack another willow branch
into a dam, creating a pond
where there had been only
a meandering stream
speckled with brown trout seconds before.
Or at least, the idea of a stream with trout,
for as soon as God set things in motion,
they took on a life of their own.
The young buck, his antlers in first velvet,
moves up the moonlit canyon,
the waves crash against the cliff's face,
a perfect yellow rose blooms by a brick wall.
You take my hand. You smile.
Every moment is the first moment.

Olive L. Sullivan

The Blue Inside

The blue of the Aegean Sea,
is heartbreakingly clear.
Blue is in me and surrounds me.
Each rock I see is a bright mosaic shard on the sea floor,
each creature a god of its own universe,
each shell an artifact of a distant culture.

The blue inside me and around me
fills my internal horizon
like the ocean meets the sky.
The farther you go,
the deeper the hue.
But where is my clarity?

I am one earthquake away
from becoming an island.
I feel my bones shifting.

As Darkness Falls

> *Somewhere over the rainbow,*
> *bluebirds fly and the dreams that you dare to —*
> *oh why, oh why can't I?*
> "Over the Rainbow/What a Wonderful World,"
> as sung by Israel "Iz" Kama Kawiwo'ole

At the horizon, ocean fades into sky.
Pink-tinted clouds blossom and
everything blue crimsons,
sea and sky reflecting one another
as darkness falls.

I nestle into your shoulder.
We watch the driftwood sparks burning holes
in the velvet indigo sky,
carry the music of the ukulele
out across the whispering sea.

Iz calls up the sky and the ocean,
the night and the crimson clouds.
Home and *far away* melt into one another
like the sky and the sea.
He calls up Kansas bluebirds,
a rainbow for them to soar over,
hope and the dream of peace
and a wonderful world.

There's an ocean and half a continent to Kansas,
where, later, we'll watch the winter sky from the
  snowy shore
of an old strip mining pit.
The water's face reflects the sky fire.
Black trees lace land to water.

Olive L. Sullivan

A great blue heron makes
its way across the lake.

On our way home,
we startle a herd of deer who fly
across the stubble cornfield,
their tails white banners
sailing into the darkening sky.

Fool's Gold

I would have told you how
the way that point of light
reflected off the water, yet
filtered down through gold then brown
then greeny depths, and
the way that oak leaf fell
and floated off out of the light
made my skin ache.

But I knew you wouldn't get it.
I knew you wouldn't see
how the pebbles lay
dry and dull on the shore
but flash sparks of mica and fool's gold
when they hit the creek.
You'd just see the Coors bottle
by the low-water bridge,
the way the silt from the sewage treatment plant
clouds up the tea-brown stream.
You can't see past the devastation.
Cow Creek is the center of the universe,
but you don't think that way.

Olive L. Sullivan

The Things We Know

Mary said *how'd you know*
that was a red-tailed hawk?
and I said I just do,
I recognize it,
like I know my face in the mirror
and my granddaughter's smile,
the way I know the sycamore from the oak
by its fruit and the color and texture of its bark.
I've always known.

I imagine my mother
turning up the lily-pad leaf
of the may apple to show the waxy bloom,
placing my hand on the rough bark,
saying *oak*, and *sycamore*.
She taught me not to be afraid
of black snakes sunning themselves
on a rock beside the creek.
This is what I know.
But it's not the same as truth,
my truth not the same as another's.

We measure out justice in lopsided sheaves,
bundle folk in one bale or another.
The darker the skin, the thicker it has to grow, and
the truths they know are not the same
as the inalienable ones I was taught to hold self-
evident.

Objective fact
is rendered insignificant
by the widespread blue above the Flint Hills.
It's just a herd of cattle

Wandering Bone

headed for the slaughterhouse,
the field mouse that the red-tailed hawk
sees as he wheels above,
staticky Patsy Cline on the radio
as I turn up one gravel road
and then another a mile on.

I scrape my knuckles on the bare wood doorframe
as hens scrabble around my feet.
I offer the farmer the hard reality
of half a dozen silver coins
 in exchange for
a dozen fresh-laid eggs,
round and white and solid
and as true as Sunday breakfast on the table.

Facts are supposed to be immutable
but truth is the hard flint bones
piercing the prairie's tawny hide,
a mirage on a hot highway,
like the dreams we remember
but cannot understand.

Olive L. Sullivan

Family Bed

Polished mahogany,
newlywed bedstead
gleaming in the back of a beat-up buckboard
all the way from St. Louis
to the Oklahoma prairie.
Not much: headboard,
footboard carved like the coach of a sleigh.
Homestead bedstead.
Thick red Russian quilts don't show
the stains of childbed —
nor deathbed stains, neither.

Now the bed's in Denver
covered with neon coral-colored sheets
and on Sundays a tangle of
bony legs and knobby little knees —
And over this sweet jumble of our limbs is
Grandma Larson's memory quilt,
her daddy's beard pulled snug
against my Frankie's baby chin,
and the Christmas tree
from nineteen ought-six across
our ticklish toes.

Two cats quilt us all together,
fabric, flesh, sinew, bone and bed,
bedstead stitched fast with
their quick-pointing quilting feet,
their tabby tails tucked in around our shoulders.
Homestead, bedstead, bedrock, cats and all —
family bed.

Family Photos

The last time I remember talking to you,
you were wearing your purple silk dress,
your white hair twisted by the wind
that seemed would blow you over.
You had the little rocking chair in your hand
and you asked me who was stealing your things,
why my dad wouldn't let you go home.
I was twelve. There was nothing I could do
but carry the chair and take you back inside with me
to the house we shared, even though you didn't
  recognize it.

The last time I saw you, in your satin-lined coffin,
my mother was wearing a red dress.
She said it was your happy day —
you were free, no longer confused,
no longer afraid.

When you died, I thought,
well, that's me, no more stories, no more history,
but I can't look through a photo album without you
leaning over my shoulder.

Years later, racked with sorrow and confusion,
my marriage flying to pieces,
my heart in chunks of ash and ice and searing fire
  and helpless,
I passed an old woman in the parking lot at King
  Soopers
holding a bag of groceries.
She looked lost. The wind rocked her,
wrapped her purple silk dress around her frail legs.
I came back to ask if she needed help

Olive L. Sullivan

and you looked out of her eyes and told me
everything would be all right.

This photo shows Thanksgiving dinner, circa 1940,
twenty-some years before I will be born.
Everyone's around the table —
that's me in your sepia flowered dress —
there's my face.
Another photo: there's you and Grandpa on the
   beach
with Jack and Mabel, Roy and Virginia,
Grace and Clifford. Your dress, wet from the surf,
is plastered against your knees.
Virginia wears a daring bathing suit with short
   sleeves
and a ruffled neckline. I see it still so clearly,
but when I was back in Galveston last year,
only the postcards would reminisce with me.

Now I am a grandmother.
My grandbaby too looks out of that 1940s
   Thanksgiving photo —
she's standing by my side wearing the body of a
   nine-year-old boy.
Face, eyes, dreams, names — the bones remember.

Blue

Robins' eggs
Kansas skies
baby blanket soft as down
and the eyes of the baby
worn denim jeans you stole
from your first boyfriend
handmade socks in different sizes
because you just learned how to knit
Grandma's turquoise bracelet
the surface of a farm pond like a mirror
on a still day
bachelor's buttons
wrapping paper and curling ribbon
prom shoes and bridesmaids' dresses
honeymoon luggage
notebooks for the first day of school
hair ribbons, bandanas
hand-painted chairs with wicker seats and
cabbage roses on the cushions
a lovely mottled fountain pen
that was my grandfather's
and the pool of ink it leaks
all over my hands
wild flowers in the spring
a woman's smoky alto voice
and the pulse of the piano behind it,
a saxophone crying out its lonesome soul
the color of the sky at midnight
Italian tile and the flash
of cobalt from a broken bottle
softened and washed up by the sea
the edges of clouds at sunrise
the ink under your skin

Olive L. Sullivan

from a cheap tattoo
shadows slipping up through
a long summer's afternoon
silky sheets at the end of a hard day
or the beginning of a holiday
or when you wake up
after the fever breaks
a new pickup truck and the eyes
of the cowboy driving it

On the Dublin-Liverpool Ferry

His kisses taste like smoke.
I am young enough to think this is a good thing,
young enough to appreciate sneaking
into the crew's quarters to make out on his bunk,
to enjoy the pitch and yaw of the ferry
and how it makes him grind harder against
my jeans-clad hips.
I am all too detached, my mind crafting
the story I'll tell about this night —
how I fled the deck, awash with rain,
the icy spray of the dark sea in my face
mingling with my forced tears,
the fierce joy of the head-high waves
breaking over the bow where I stand
pretending to be heartbroken,
how I fell into this sour bed because
I longed for the boy I left on the West Coast,
how I watched him smack his fist
into the stone wall of the station
as my train pulled out for Dublin,
how I vowed to come back,
the yearning song of return
all us children of Irish immigrants
learn in the cradle.
My passionate declarations taste like ash as I
move from his farewell embrace
to the smoky kisses of a sailor
I will never see again either.
I am old enough now to know that is a good thing.

Olive L. Sullivan

November Falling

Watch the birds furl and unfurl across the prairie,
the tawny flash of a dog's flank
as she harries the stubble fields for rabbits and field mice.
Look at the way the slant winter light falls,
how the lake carries only the memory of blue.

I carry your anger like a rucksack
heavy with six pounds of self-help books —
but you've forgotten the water and the matches.

Standing by the carcass of a deer,
mired in the mud of the borrow ditch,
it's hard to remember the sky.

The Black Dog
(after C.D. Wright)

Black dog, he chase me all the way from Rosedale
to the Fox Town city limits.

Two white horses side by side
in a front yard in Arcadia, Kansas.

goat eating the porch railing

Rain. Rain. Granny on the rooftop nailing on shingles,
biceps bunching and releasing, sleek as polished bone.

White. I see white swans.

The black dog won't leave me alone.

Jukebox in the living room, bootleg in the Packard's
   trunk.
She smashed the odometer so Buddy wouldn't know
she'd been running hooch again.

Bathtub gin. Angels on the roof,
their wings white like polished bone.

She kept the family dog, big black hound. Darksome.
Gleam of red eyes. Moonshine.

Starshine. Darkshine. A chainsaw. Dogs
lapping the blood.

Black dog licking the oil from my fingers.

Tuesday. Calendar says springtime. Crocuses.
Covered in falling snow, flakes like white swans like

swallows of moonshine. Barn swallows.
The white bathtub. Gin clear as spring

Water.

Olive L. Sullivan

Did you know, in Kazahkstan, vodka only costs seven
  bucks a bottle?
Is as clear as spring? My name was Natasha.

But my black dog — the Irish women bared their breasts
to tame the bloodlust of the Hound of Ulster.

Black dog laps my heart from my fingertips.

Fox Town City Limits — wanna go see Papa Roach
play tonight?

Shrimp. Fresh tomatoes. Bait. Milk.

I see. Oh I see.

The black dog follows me.

Nay, it is a swan, a swan.

In Arcadia, nymphs dance in the forest.
The gods pursue them like hounds. They melt
into the white sky like snow.

In Acadia, the word for *cook* is the same as
the word *cayenne*. Darksome. The black god.

The black dog roams the cypress swamp.
howls *I see I see.*

I know. I was there. In the orange groves.

The family dog is Cuchulain. We
bare our breasts. The dog laps our blood.

The angels carry chainsaws. Nay,
it is a swan.

The jukebox in the corner. Floorboards
tremble like a bride. The jukebox.
I lead you willingly along the darksome.
Paths. I lead you. I follow

the black dog follows me to Rosedale.
How do I look? I have forgotten.

Do you remember Meg and the jam?
In Rosedale. We would be happy. We were.
Aren't we?

Beautiful things fill every vacancy.

I was there. I know. I saw.

The white horses. Black dog.
Misty rain. An electric fence.

He was thrown to the ground under the power.

Electroshock. The chainsaw. Therapy.
For the black dog. It knows now that horses can spit
  fire.

Their velvet noses. Their perfect nostrils.
God rested. The black dog

weeping. I plant yellow marigolds
in the front yard. A goat eats them.

The squirrels dig up the tulip bulbs, trade them in
for black walnut trees. The black dog. Howls.

I plant beautiful things in every vacancy.

Grave a curse on my back. It will never wash off.
We danced every night.

We dance. Didn't we? The jukebox?
The black dog?

Nay, it is a swan, a swan.

I see. Oh, I see.

Olive L. Sullivan

Baghdad

I woke up when your
burned body thumped to the tile
outside my door,
four stories down from the balcony
of your commandeered palace.
Out my window a pall of smoke
covers the ruined fairytale face of Baghdad,
domes of mosques rising like mushroom clouds.
At home, the president hands me
a folded triangle, rags to commemorate your
service to our nation.
It's all I can do not to spit in his face.

Requiem on a November Night

We come around the curve above Center Creek,
tumble into a jeweler's scrapbox —
grass a handful of copper wire
strewn across a jumble of brass,
sumac leaves, oaks, sycamore
fluxing through all the hues of copper oxidizing,
red ruby heat of nickel in the forge,
pure gold of cottonwood leaves
splashed against the enamel sky,
the creek a rope of bronze
still dimpled from its forging.

Police lights gleam
against wet pavement.
Radio squawks winter storm alert.
A baby-faced officer waves us past
the slick of oil on wet tarmac,
past white faces of the witnesses,
stark as scattered leaves.
Rain spits against the window shield,
turning to sleet as it falls.

***

Irina faces her reflection
in the rain-dark window,
cocks her elbow and listens
for the crash of the piano intro
in her mind.
She snaps the first bitter notes
from her viola's strings,
bowing Hindemith, sobbing,
into the darkness.

Olive L. Sullivan

She watches her own face
above the black dress in the black window,
her back arching at the unaccustomed stress
of her too-high concert heels.
She bends her head.
The bow dips.
Dark music fills her little house.

***

Irina's sister aims her torch
at the strips of copper pinned
at right angles on her tiny forge.
Blue flame licks at the snips of solder and flux,
the metal glowing orange, pulsing into crimson
until, in a blink,
the silver solder flows along the joint
like the tear sliding down Irina's face.

Oblivion Tango

Guitar and piano
whisper in the corner,
lonely as layers of dust.

My calluses have softened,
cradled in your palm.

You are the fixed foot,
the steadfast sun at the center
of my wayward orbit,
but the moon
still circles me alone.

I pluck the guitar,
pick notes falling
into a minor chord.

My fingertips
start to bleed.

Olive L. Sullivan

Wandering Bone

Oh, Willie, don't you know I've always been
a rolling stone, a rolling stone,
don't you know I've just been searching,
just searching for a place I can call my home?
Oh, Willie, don't you know, I thought you'd be the one,
the one who gave me a reason not to roam.

But oh, I got that wandering bone,
I'm a wandering bone, a wandering bone.
Don't need no place to call my home.

But, oh, Willie, don't you know I don't want to be alone.
I need you to be the one who makes me feel at home.
I don't want to spend my life like a rolling stone,
a rolling stone.
Please give me just one reason, just one reason,
to call this sorry place my home.

But oh, I got that wandering bone,
I'm a wandering bone, a wandering bone.
Don't need no place to call my home.

I need to drive on down the highway,
need to follow that old white line.
I need to see the skies in far-off places,
need to wake up far away, far away
from these sad and lonely times.
I want to find somewhere, somewhere,
somewhere that feels like home,
don't want to die a woman with a wandering bone.

Oh, Willie, don't you see, don't you see how hard I've tried?
Don't you see how close I am to moving on?
Just give me one small reason, just one reason
to call this sorry place my home.

Think Stars, Count Sheep

I think I'm gonna be sick —
Don't think about it.
Think stars, count sheep,
remember kicking through oak leaves
searching for the first violets in spring,
or every morning lifting green umbrella tops
of mayflowers until one day
you find the waxy blossom
like a lily on a pond.
What happened after that?
What moved the days
past June and through July, or
did time lay empty as the moment
making love slides into sleep, and
you lie staring at the ceiling
whispering the litany:
Don't think about it.
Think stars, count sheep.
Don't listen to him snore.

Olive L. Sullivan

Divorcing

Is there any hope?
We sit at the table in silence.
The simplest phrases tilt
at cross purposes. I wield
the butter knife, you slice
the vicious bread.

Talking of the ripe tomatoes and the corn,
my hands flutter out and up,
a kestrel straining at the jesses.
They twist away, ball into
fists, deny my mask —
they snap and
coil down and
the kestrel shoots screaming
into the sky. Larks
fall like words, hang
heavy in the air like
the weight of your hand on my back
in the middle of the night
when I pretend to be sleeping.

Landslip

If I were a planet,
continents would be shifting.
Mountain ranges would rise and flux
and sink again, and
lava would flow hot
and thick. I'm volcanic.
I'm tectonic plates shifting
into new forms. Let me tell you,
being molten is hard work.
But now that the old mold's broken,
I can't wait to see
which way the rivers run
when the landslip ends.

Olive L. Sullivan

Green How I Want You

> Verde que te quiero verde.
> Verde viento. Verdes ramas.
> — Federico García Lorca

Green how I want you green,
my paddle dipping
into moss-colored water,
flashing green scales
of a bass struggling on your line.

Brown how I want you brown,
your eyes, laugh-crinkled,
catching mine, message passed
as surely as a note
in high school Spanish class.

Blue how I want you blue,
atop the castle walls at Peñafiel,
nothing but sky supporting you.

Black how I want you black,
marks on printed pages
binding us like a folio,
the words we make to play.

Red how I want you red,
evergreen passion flaring in your brown eyes,
blue coverlet tossed back,
book set aside —
red how I want you red.

Winter Down

First cool evening,
there are still fireflies
and mosquitoes,
but we build a fire,

scraps of paper
tucked into a teepee
of twigs, then
flying up like stars

following each other
into the cool dark,
wordless poems
written on ash.

~

Awake in the dark,
the roar of rain on the roof,
your solid back
pushes against mine.

Lend me your arm,
wrap me in eiderdown,
whisper poems
into my sleeping ear.

~

A snowbound world
dawns gray and silent.
The tracks of deer and
chickadee await.

Come down to my room
and bring the dogs.
Bring a good book.
Winter down with me.

Olive L. Sullivan

The Edge of the Map

Half a World Away

There's no one here to show me the stars,
no one to slip his arm around my shoulders,
lift my hand and steer it gently to the south, the west,
until Sirius pops into view from nothingness,
a minor miracle, and then another.

Show me the sky where you are tonight,
the huntsman and the Southern Cross,
skies a half a world away from home.
It's raining there, the red dirt streets
slick and shiny with it. Here

it's cold, the first scarlet leaves of fall
cling to wet black tarmac, and the air
smells like wood smoke.

Your scent surrounds me.
My heart beats, once, twice.
Beside me, the dog moans in her sleep,
and this bed is a continent of sorrow.

Olive L. Sullivan

The Black Dog Follows

I ran away from home
for the weekend. Carried
a pen, two notebooks, three books to read
a ream of paper, words printed
and scratched out. Turquoise
ink corrections interleaving images.

I brought the black dog with me too.
He won't leave me alone.
He presses his spine against me
in the bed at night.
Memory foam holds our shapes like
forensic casts. His soft snores are moans.
Sorrow fills my dreams.

Regret is my morning tea.
Snow covers the first spring crocuses.
The clock is out of time.
I turned the a/c on at bedtime;
the heater kicked in at dawn.
My ragg wool socks pad across the floor
like wolves' silent paws.

The black dog's nails click
against the linoleum like knitting needles
flashing back and forth creating
a fabric entirely made up of holes.
I ran away from home.

But it followed me here. Time has run
out. The black dog.

La Lupa

When I found them there on the banks of the Tiber,
the others said to leave them be. Said —
they smelled like danger. Said —
I should snap their necks and go on home.
But all I could see was their hairless innocence,
skin pink as the newborn noses on my own small pups.
Their mewling caused my milk to flow,
and I knew that I could save them.

I carried each boy in my jaws,
let them nurse next to their sisters,
watched them tumble and play outside the den
in the autumn sunshine.

I knew someday one of them would grow to manhood,
plunge a knife into my throat,
wear my pelt for warmth upon his shoulders.
Forever after he would fear the wild night
and lock himself indoors. But my second son,
who would not weep for me,
would step outside on nights with a full moon,
and when his sisters called,
he would open wide his throat and answer.

Olive L. Sullivan

Avebury

We tramped until
the sky turned purple
and the sheep glowed
like ghosts among the
standing stones. We
fenced crazily
with tent poles
then went inside
to sleep next to
the barrows of dead kings
and I said
what if our souls were
unattached,
and watching us?

The Galapagos Blue-Foot Strut

I show you my bright blue feet,
you show me yours.
We dance in the lava fields,
our wings outspread
and reaching skyward
as we sway and strut
and tap our beautiful feet.
You braid my downy feathers with your beak.
You bring me twigs — delightful!

The other machos whistle,
show me their feet,
offer to dance, bowing as they
lay their sticks before me —
none have feet so finely blue,
none have twigs so supple.

It's Twig Month,
the last dry weeks before the world
bursts into green and yellow blossom.
Let us dance and strut in the black lava field.
Let us build our nest
where the turquoise ocean sings.

Olive L. Sullivan

Barqerizo Moreño

My newly browned skin
tastes of salt,
glitters with flecks of golden sand
from the beach on Floreana Island
where pirates and sea captains
left their love letters
and green sea turtles mate in the surf.

A man called Carlos
wraps my hair in red and turquoise thread,
anchors it with a silver bead
and a tiger's eye.
He calls me Alex, and I am
irrevocably altered.

A year later, a nurse
will snip off that silver bead,
hand me a backless paper gown
and slide me into the sterile tube
of the MRI machine.

When I close my eyes,
dolphins lead my ship to sea.
The ocean rocks me to sleep
under the unfamiliar stars.

Weekend Away

I wake in snowy woods I've never walked before,
the air so sharp and cold
it seems to slice one breath from the next.
Words, isolated puffs of vapor
fall and shatter on the unfamiliar ground.

Gone the trees I know like sisters,
replaced by birches pale against the dark
like swaying dryads, willows along a creek
where an unseen raccoon washes his invisible dinner.

Three women have traveled with me
to a city where we see
a man making snow to cover a moonlit mountain,
where we look out windows in the sky
at towers glittering under a pale sun
slanting at an unfamiliar angle.

Sometimes we are sisters, sometimes I their mother,
sometimes alien even to ourselves.
We live by our wits, cover ourselves in new skins,
trailing scarves and incense through our dreams.

Sidewalks paved with marble
carry us where a woman with light colored eyes leads us
through a maze, speaking rapidly a language
none of us knows, but that makes us laugh.

A troll asks us music trivia, but lets us pass.
We eat the food we are offered
and find ourselves again traveling.
The landscape shifts like a mythic beast
shuddering his hoary skin

Olive L. Sullivan

under our strange footsteps,
and when it settles once again,
we are back within our own home watershed
and it is Monday morning.

The Wisdom of the Staircase

Angry words, a biting retort, and the slam of a door
at the top of the steep narrow stairs,
the rattling flight that leaves
a hollow in the pit of my stomach and
halfway down, more measured steps
as I regret the things I have not said.
Faced with the stark geometry of riser and tread
I grip the banister to keep from falling,
long for the curve of your hand around mine,
regret the sharp jerk of my head as you bend to kiss my ear,
the way I spurn your open palm.
The wisdom of the staircase pools around me
with the smell of cabbage cooking, garlic and onions,
the whispering of all the tender things
I meant to say instead.

Olive L. Sullivan

The Edge of the Map

Our hearts swell with wonder
as we cross the blank edge of the map.
We see strange mountains.
We ford each new river.

At all that's offered to us,
we gather handfuls of gratitude.
We ford each new river
carrying nothing but dreams.

We gather handfuls of gratitude
as we cross the Continental Divide
carrying nothing but dreams.
We count the black bear, the eagle, the elk.

We cross the Continental Divide.
Spread before us is a new country.
We count the black bear, the eagle, the elk.
The juice of wild berries runs down our chins.

Spread before us is a new country,
the ocean like a dream on the horizon.
The juice of wild berries runs down our chins.
We throw away our box of maps.

The ocean like a dream on the horizon,
river racing us to the delta,
we throw away our box of maps
and dash into the crashing surf.

River racing us to the delta,
we drive into the setting sun.
We throw away our box of maps.
The road is the one thing binding us together.

Tortugero

Harboring sea turtles
as they lay
their eggs on the black sand beach,
iguana, a gecko basking
on my shower wall,
frogs breeding in the swimming pool —
Tortugero holds
a seething, fecund mélange
like the beginning of the world,
each an echo of the universe complete.

Seen magnified by fifty thousand times,
the gecko's toes are tiny fertile forests,
the eggs the frogs lay are galaxies and suns,
each grain of black sand
a granite boulder
the turtles pack
around the fresh clutch
of leathery eggs,
the interstices
between each grain
as empty as the space
between this world and its moon.

Would Tortugero, seen from fifty thousand light
years out,
seem nothing more, or less,
than the iguana's patterned flesh?

Olive L. Sullivan

What the Mosquito Said

The mosquito sings to my ear,
I love you!
How delicious you are!
Let me kiss you!
and in kissing,
leaves a love bite
that for days
will remind me of her courtship.

The Ibo people, in old stories,
say the mosquito once loved the ear,
but when she pressed her suit,
Ear laughed.
Look at you!
You are so delicate and frail,
you will be dead soon.
Why should I marry you?
Of course the mosquito,
mother of dengue and malaria,
did not die —
and ever after, she sings to the ear,
I'm still here.

She thrives at the bend of the river
in flood season, where
the Paraguay has burst its banks
and turned city streets and slums
into canals and swamps.
Oreja! Te amo! she sings,
Dejame besarte otra vez.
Let me kiss you again.

Alas, there is a third party
in this love triangle —
the mosquito, the ear,
and the hand,
who cries, *Basta!*
Enough!
And *Slap!*
And *Squish!*
and the ear hears only a faint ringing.

The love song of the mosquito ends,
as all good stories do,
from Sophocles to Achebe to Garcia Marquez,
in a smear of blood.

Olive L. Sullivan

June 12 in Paraguay

In the street underneath my hotel window,
someone is
playing an old Edith Piaf record,
laughing,
speaking quick Spanish
with the shush and slur of
South America.
Someone else
plays a quick snatch of bossa nova,
and the kids down the street
turn up the car stereo,
treating all of us
to American hip-hop.
A cat in heat is yowling.
A shoeshine boy
tells his customer
he's hungry,
his home is flooded,
it's his birthday,
he would like to have an *hamburgesa*.
He argues for a bigger tip.

At the carnival
on the Costanera tonight
spotlights spike
the gray night sky
as the deep bass beat
of the main attraction
pulses through our soles.
It's a holiday,
another celebration
of another war,
the survivors and descendants

making heroes and martyrs
of the dead,
those scared cold boys who,
in the desert north,
drank their own urine,
filtered through *mate* leaves.
The concert goers,
with their *termos* y *guampas*,
drink the cold *mate* tea,
the *tereré*,
and think they
are honoring their heroes,
but the dead
stay dead.

Back home,
there's talk of another war,
US troops sent to Iraq.
This poem
could have been written
in 1990,
or 2003,
or maybe
1915,
when British troops
occupy the desert
with the Russians
and the sand.
People keep
asking me to justify
American foreign policy,
to explain
what the president thinks,

Olive L. Sullivan

but I don't have the grammar to answer,
even if I had the heart.

Squatting in a ragged camp
at the abandoned train station,
a boy with a guitar
strums an old Pete Seeger song:
When will they ever learn?
When will they ever learn?

This is what I want to say to the world:
Go home. Hug your children.
Give your mother a kiss.
The world
can look out for itself
another day.
If you have a home,
go there.
Count your blessings,
then count again.

Barrio San Jeronimo

> *No hay inundacion.*
> —Alfredo Benitz, CEO of the Social Department of
> Asunción, Paraguay, reported by the IPS July 7, 2014

It's raining in Brazil,
sending churning brown water
over the dam at Itaipu.
It pours into the devil's throat
to swallow the cataracts at Iguazu,
and all its tourism industry.

It takes six months
for the floodwaters
to reach Asunción,
but now the kids
in el Barrio San Jeronimo
are splashing in the streets.
From the top of the café
we can see the whole tattered city,
tile rooftops, church towers,
failed high rises,
the bay and the river
creeping up the roads
and lapping at the bright green doorsteps.

In the shade
behind the café's turquoise iron gate,
los mujeres, Aleli y Teodosia,
laugh and tell stories
about *el sasquatch*,
the *pie grande* from Georgia
they saw on the Discovery Channel.
When Teodosia laughs,
she covers her mouth

Olive L. Sullivan

to hide her missing teeth.
When she says *Flor EE da*,
the i soars high like a tropical bird.
When I say it back — *yes, FLOR uh duh*,
the syllables thunk
like an axe blade into a stump,
and its echo.

The kids are playing *futbol*
on the rooftop —
in the US it would be a pickup game
of basketball in the hood —
the two faces of the Paraguayan flag
a backdrop
to San Jeronimo's
own little piece of the World Cup.
More rain clouds are moving down from Brazil,
but Teodosia is still laughing.

Ghost City

From the rooftop you can see
it's a city of ghosts —
abandoned gardens,
dead buildings,
windows empty holes,
black mildew like graffiti
painting the yellow walls,
sculpted cornucopias
crumbling to component dust.
Only the stray dogs
at the shanty town
by the river still move,
white shadows slinking
along the *malecón*
where lovers strolled
holding hands above the colonial river.
Now, garbage and feral children,
cats and pigeons claim the streets.

Olive L. Sullivan

The Heart of Giocalto

> *for Dennis Olsen*
> *Dec. 2, 1941-Nov. 26, 2015*

The music is shut off,
the guitar case closed.
The strings of the mandolin are muted
and his whistle's silenced.

Our voices are hushed as we leave the sickroom.
We thank the hospice volunteer,
blink tears from our heavy lashes.
There will, we know, be more tears.
Giocalto will be bleak and cold this winter
without its beating heart.

Next summer, though, we'll gather
on the loggia over *prosciutto e melone*,
pass brightly patterned bowls of pasta,
plates of grilled lamb. We'll laugh,
we'll hold hands, we'll clink our glasses
of prosecco, say *cin-cin* and *salud* and *sláinte*,
all words meaning *health* and *I love you*.

There may be tears as well —
we knew they'd come —
but when the dogs begin to bark
as evening falls across the valley
and the first stars come out
over the Apennine hills,
I hope we'll find the courage
once again to sing —
the song about the fox and the gray goose,
the song about Laredo.

Wandering Bone

That's how we'll honor him,
the soul of Giocalto — gone to us,
but part of the very structure
of its stones.

Olive L. Sullivan

The Bone Goddess

I followed you upstairs,
you and the Bone Goddess,
and it wasn't until
she turned her head towards me
that I saw, really saw, you.

She is my enemy,
the Bone Goddess, and
she is my salvation.
She is indestructible,
inscrutable, and the key
to all knowing.

When you were with me,
my face masked her skull
and my flesh padded
out her thighs and hips and belly.

Now when her black eyes
pierce my soul, my own eyes
fly open. Now when I
look at you, I see ash
instead of flame —
not even dying embers or betrayal

because behind your velvet eyes,
behind that grin I loved,
she's always been there,
the Bone Goddess,
the one I didn't want to face,
didn't want to recognize —
the one I now embrace.

Carrying Darkness

I've been places you can't even begin to imagine
dark places
places where maybe once
someone laughed,
but it was a choked laugh
full of dust, the dust
composed of
cells of skin, salt, blood, and bits of bone
graveyard dust in the palm of a *voodouienne*.
I've been places you don't want to see,
places where I wrote curses on my skin in black and
ocher,
the colors of the south wind that carries death,
and nailed them to the wall of the prison cell
with a Valentine's Day rose.
You wouldn't know it to talk to me but
I carry them with me.
Sometimes when I least expect it
the darkness seeps through the soles of my feet,
the crown of my head, an elbow —
pools around me like a black velvet cape,
like a jaguar lying in wait,
like drowning in a cypress swamp. Like that.
Be glad you don't get it.
It's not the kind of thing you want to survive.

Olive L. Sullivan

Foreign Places

I come to you from another country,
the one you enter when you sleep and dream
or when you die, and
I walk toward you down
the airport hallway with the dust
of foreign places glittering
on my feet, an incense
of cool wind and far off bells
trailing behind me and
sifting from my hair like snow.
My speech is full of the cadence
of others' tongues,
Spanish and Lakota,
a Texas drawl and
the seeds of jazz
fall from my lips, salsa
is on my tongue and in my walk.
I see your face, the fear
at seeing I am not
the one who left here,
that foreign spaces have
transformed me.
I am Mexican now, or Lakota,
and my green eyes and sandy hair
cannot belie that
powerful renewal of becoming truer
to that true dream self,
of becoming Mexican and Lakota and
more and more myself.

Pilgrimage

Incense makes me sneeze, and
the sunlight spikes
from one gray column to another.
The cool stone benches
make my back hurt.

Pilgrims kiss the scalloped shoulders
of the statue of St. James, offer
their blistered and bruised feet,
their battered tennis shoes.

My feet are tired, too. A basso voice
soars above the treble of the boys' choir.
A woman with a white cane
struggles up the stony steps.

I wear the shell of Santiago
on a cord around my neck
but in my backpack I carry pebbles
from a shingled beach in Á Coruña.

There, the sea licked my toes,
kissed my thighs, and sighed.
Venus offered her bright light
above the tower of Hercules,
pointing our path home to Madrid.

We picnic by a nameless castle
in the valley of the Sil
and I show you a shell
shaped like the moon we saw from Toro.

A woman drives seven honey-colored cows
up a steep hill toward red-tiled roofs

Olive L. Sullivan

and dares us with flashing black eyes
to take her photo.

Pilgrims pass us on their way to Santiago,
but we carry our own blessings home.

Election Year

Back home, the candidates are talking
about building walls.
The police complain that
everyone hates them.
In Hungary, they're erecting razor wire.
Dazed refugees stumble across another border.
They've pulled dead children from the churning surf.
Now they reach for bottles of water,
bread, a place to rest.
Government troops push them onward.
They're someone else's problem now.

Across the indigo waters of the strait those
immigrants crossed in leaky boats,
men smash white marble monuments,
erasing this inconvenient history,
warped mirror of the stone saints
Cromwell's men beheaded half a millennium ago.

Flipping *us* and *them* doesn't heal our
fresh-made wounds.
Blinding another man won't give me back
my sight.
Have we — collectively — learned nothing
that can hold us up, all of us,
without requiring that someone else
be ground down?

What if we lifted our faces
from the texts of ancient books?
Instead of arguing whose god is supreme,
what if we looked into one another's eyes?
What if I offered you a juicy peach?

Olive L. Sullivan

What if we then clasped each other's
sweet, sticky palms?
What if, together, we carried the children,
the grandmothers, the babies, to safety?

The Angel of Nagasaki

She covers her stony eyes with marble palms.
When the bomb falls,
she sees her blood through neon eyelids,
the bones of her hand like a crimson x-ray.
The thunderclap is the shout of a god,
the bitter wind his breath.

She opens her eyes to a sky washed white,
surrounded by the rubble of her cathedral.
Around her she sees nothing but shadows,
the shadow of a little boy on his way to school,
flattened on the sidewalk —
the shadow of a nun on the sole wall still standing.

The angel spreads her wings, rises
over the wasteland of her adopted homeland.
She scatters a thousand paper cranes across the sky.
Resting against a stone wall, she sees a Russian solider.
He lights a cigarette, ruffles the silky ears of his German
    shepherd,
the dog a soldier too.

How the angel wishes she could weep!
Her stone eye sockets are empty and dry as dust.
She longs for the salt erosion of tears,
but all she sees is the image
of her crimson bones against
her own boiling neon blood.

The winds of Nagasaki carry ashes
over the East China Sea, west and north,
fluttering over Moscow, over divided Berlin.
The angel knows these ashes

Olive L. Sullivan

are what's left of Truman's letter
to the Soviets — that the remains of Nagasaki
are his warning of what could come to be.

At her new post in the peace garden in Paris,
the angel of Nagasaki opens one sightless eye,
gazes at this dream of peace
grown up through the aftermath of war.
Leaves flutter like paper cranes over her head
and she wonders again how come
eighty thousand souls became ash in an instant
so the president could post this warning.
She prays unceasingly, her eyes burned
from her broken marble face,
that her new home, rocked
with terrorist attacks, a babel of languages, fear and
    mistrust,
will not become the reply:
that Truman's letter will not be returned
with postage due.

The Bulls of Marroquin y Macias, The Bulls of Armillita

Bravely fighting, bravely dying,
blood and dust and flowers flying —
outlawed in the name of kindness.
Gone the bull ring, gone the matador,
gone the pomp and gone the glory,
bulls no longer bred for battle
but in feedlots fattening, dying.

All that lingers are the memories
mounted on the walls above us,
heads and photos long forgotten,
faded as the silvered mirror,
and the sons of Marroquin y Macias,
the sons of Armillita
make their wages other ways, but
dream of daring days of story.

Olive L. Sullivan

Spain Wins the World Cup, 2010

The bear in the Puerta del Sol
kisses the madrone tree in exultation.
I follow you down narrow, winding streets
until we come upon a plaza
full of Madrileños
waving flags of red and gold against the dying sun.

Above us, angels peer down from the rooftops,
their marble faces as placid as a Kansas lily pond.
McDonald's balcony is packed with *futbol* fans,
the Spanish claiming its red and gold as their own.
Like little bulls, the children ride their parents'
shoulders
to cheer the city's newest heroes home.
All of Madrid turns out
to fill the streets with song.

Souvenir

Saffron, turmeric, cayenne, cinnamon —
a spice rack full of the exotic,
colors tease the eyes,
aromas and flavors zap the tongue,
the best of them unnoticed at first,
then blossoming into wonder

like a blue pottery bowl
tucked behind the mangoes displayed
at the back of a stall in the bazaar.

You stumble, dazed by relentless sunlight,
shoved by people in white robes and headscarves,
stunned by the sun and the dust and the music
of camel bells, the muzzeins' ululating
call to prayer.

Hunkered in the cool shade,
your eyes adjust to darkness
and the bowl beckons,
a deep azure the color of Kansas skies
when you lay on your back
between the rows of towering corn.

So you turn away from the bright bangles
and painted leather bags and boots,
and barter your last piastre for the thing
that reminds you most of home.

Olive L. Sullivan

The Seventh Year

That's how it started —
driving across Kansas on a wave of the blues,
poems working their way to the surface
bearing messages of stone and fern,
soul and bone and dirt.
The seventh year is the one when
everything changes — you've seen it coming
like a tornado on the horizon.
The sky turns black and yellow and green,
you run for the storm cellar
and play gin rummy on a rickety card table
next to the canned goods,
then sleep piled on the floor like puppies.
When birds carol the new day,
the sky like a basket of clean cotton towels,
nothing has changed but
everything is new.

Sunset on Lake Michigan

The sand glistens
under the gray susurrations
below the pewter sky.
When the rain stops we
count aspen, dividing them by spruce
to discover the price of gold.
The tide like ice slips out to meet the sea,
copper curls chase bronze along the swell of a sunlit wave,
surf spills sacrifice onto the sand.
For weeks my words
are full of the cadence of yours.

Olive L. Sullivan

Driving West

This isn't a poem about the blue clouds
like out of focus angels
that we saw just south of Lawrence,
nor about the way we came up
over the rise east of Manhattan
and found the Flint Hills spread before us —
nor the sunset that carried every bit
of grain and speck of dust
into a silver-edged symphony
of gold and neon, and it's not
the way the dying sun
lit the southwest face
of the grain elevator somewhere past Hays,
exalting it above its workaday self —
not the way the colors feel, the lace border
of black bare branches
backlit by a stripe
of orange sherbet sky,
the lake of blue clouds
like the blue shadows
caught in the drifts of snow
swelling across the prairie.
Instead, this poem is
you and me and Frank and Georgia,
crammed into a
too-small car with too much stuff
arguing the politics of the Civil War
and taking turns
to sit in the less crowded front seat,
where we can move our feet
without being snarled in blankets
and book bags and the laptop's wires,
driving toward invisible mountains.

Coming Back from New Mexico at Night

It's a leap of faith for sure,
this driving across New Mexico sometimes.
In daylight it's not bad because
the roads run straight — the only curve's
a snake of road tar sliding into desert. But
then it shimmers, shifts, twists into noonday mirages:

A pool of water swirls into the sky,
or is it the sky itself? Or glass? And
you're driving up the zia's rays
onto enchanted roads to nowhere special.

At night, though, that's another story.
The old ones, los viejos, are waiting
by the road, roaming round recuerdos,
waiting for revenge or
conversation with the living.
The ghost at Seven Rivers says,
Nice car, and disappears.
Outside Las Vegas a white shape
emerges from the scrub
to hitchhike past the haunted limits
of eternal night. All around the edges
of the headlight's range
shapes shimmer, shift,
resolve themselves into
the flashing yellow coyote's eyes,
a herd of deer, a cholla's arms,
that jackrabbit frozen in the beams.
And when the road rises up into the Milky Way
you find you're flying from the edge
of mesas into darkness.

Olive L. Sullivan

Fountain of Desire

A Coruña, 2010

El *fuente de deseo*:
Bring here your dreams,
your secrets — drop a coin,
rest hot, tired feet on a cool stone bench,
tilt back your head
to the sun-dappled vault
of chestnut leaves and branches.
Hold your breath.
Make a wish.
Exchange a kiss with your companion,
then return to the hurly-burly city streets,
but carry with you
the cathedral of desire.

Gas Station Guru

The haloed lights from the Conoco look good.
They make me squint my eyes
and wish for that wispy river bottom fog
I've been driving through all night.
I'm not exactly lost, just
turned around, mixed up
somehow and
looking for some guidance.
The light and warmth and the smell
of hot dogs seep out into cool night, and
the woman behind the counter,
she says, *Hey. Mean night.*
Yeah, says I, *I'm lost.*
She glances at me sharp and says,
No, you ain't. It's just a dark patch on the way.
And I want to kneel and hug her feet,
cry out my sorrow and
let go the rigid strength that's all that holds me up,
but
like she sees my knees start bending
she snaps, *Hold on there, honey.*
I ain't your mother and I ain't
no gas station guru, but I'll
be your friend, and she loads my hands
with talismans —
beef jerky and Ding Dongs,
a package of Doritos and a large Diet Coke.
She takes my map and marks the route.
When she touches my hands,
her own are cold as ice and
she sees I know it
and she laughs, says,
This here's your way — go down
to the third light, turn left til
you hit 96, then you'll see,
you'll be home by mornin'.

Olive L. Sullivan

Everyday Mermaids

Homecoming

I've dreamed this life once before —
the easy, slow passage of days,
bright faces gathered round a dinner table,
hard work, cool at night. But
that time there wasn't this
exhaustion — this urge to sleep forever and
forever. That time everyone was
young and dreaming of tomorrow.

Olive L. Sullivan

Girl, Recovering

James says fresh air and sunshine will help.
He believes in vegetables
but scoffs at Port Reyes Station's organic market.
He should know; he's got a degree in soil science.
He's a master of compost.

After dinner, he and the restaurateur
discuss it — their conversation rich and dense
with words like *piggery, sourcing, foodshed*.
I am coughing in the parking lot.
James says my cough is not productive.

Later, he and his brother strum their guitars
and tease us when we nod off by the fireplace.
Maybe you guys should go to bed,
get some rest.

I spend the night in codeniated dreams.
The ocean breathes behind the bluff
above my headboard. All night
the wind rushes through the eucalyptus trees.

I wake under a blue and white china plate counterpane,
white sheets, white walls and ceiling that
mostly stay in place, although
the door frame has a tendency to pitch
dizzily. A four-pane windowsill,
the chickens clucking — I am
a Flemish masterpiece — girl,
recovering, with novels and high-tech devices.

James catches a rainbow trout
at Alpine Lake and we
eat it for supper with
greens from the Bolinas famers' market.
We can feel the sunlight surging
through our cells.

Rasp

After the solstice, the sun
arcs more slowly across the winter sky,
a neon coin slipping into
the glowing furnace of the west —

sweet evening light etches
the planes of your face,
the curve of your nose,
softens shadows under your tired eyes.

The rasp of stubble as you draw your hand
across your jaw causes me to catch
my breath, makes my heart skip a necessary beat.

Your square hands, capable
with kitchen knife, fishing rod, or pen,
touch my collarbone.

Each blade of golden grass stands distinct,
each bare tree branch bends toward
the lengthening light,
and the sky kisses the silver surface
of the marsh with icy blue.
The cusp of the season
signals the softening of days,
the softening of my bones,

your fingers kneading my taut muscles until I am
liquid everywhere.
My palm cups your evening beard
and my skin sighs with longing.

Olive L. Sullivan

Going to La Gruta After You Leave for Kansas

I left the warmth of your bed this morning
to walk the cobbled streets back to the old convent,
a stark white cell, dark wooden cross,
the sound of bells.

You left for the airport.
Now you're suspended in the clouds somewhere
between worlds, between languages,
between landscapes equally unique and
equally disdained, between the warmth of our bed
and the newly monastic solitude of your own.

Me, I float in the hot springs pool at La Gruta,
suspended between silence and
a torrent of foreign words,
caught between the sky and its reflection.

Kiosk

I skip a flake of stone across the water
and imagine you in Africa.
Will the noonday sun blaze so brightly
it will sear away the memory of the dawn haze
over Elk River, the deer we saw on the far shore?
When you come home, you'll be
someone else. I can reach across the table now
and hold your hand,
but you're already miles away —
on a different continent,
under a different constellation
whose light will reach me
years too late to matter.
Will our new selves
recognize the shadows?
Will they fade like postcards
at an outdoor kiosk?

Olive L. Sullivan

Smiley's Bar

The coyote made it into the poem,
but not the hummingbird,
the yellow roses,
but not the fabulous terra cotta chicken,
not the woman who spoke of herself
only in third person,
or the girl flying a kite on the beach.
Smiley's made it into the poem,
but only because of the band
and the upright bass,
the bass player cradling her neck against his jaw,
strong hands controlling each chord,
his arm curved around her waist
like that of the couple on the tiny dance floor,
his right hand pulling the strings,
her whole being throbbing from
the depths of her sylvan soul,
the beat of an old-time string band
against the ethereal melody of the New Age
setting up a tension that she can
barely endure, throbbing, throbbing, until
the A string snaps and
curls up and around his hand,
embracing him. She says, oh, oh,
and has to be carried to the back room
to lie down, her electric understudy
taking her place on stage and
changing the whole tenor of the evening,
the bass player holding it stiffly
like a boy at his first junior high school dance,
while in the back, the upright bass
throbs oh, she moans oh,
and the eucalyptus trees say hush, hush,
the sea says shhhh,
the full moon says oh, yes, oh.

Elephant Jam
(Halloween at the Elephant Room in Austin)

Streams of neon light
flow psychedelic from the drumsticks —
the saxophone bleeds indigo
into the Texas night.
Out on the purple sage,
the coyotes howl
and we, too, sing to that blue, blue moon.

I look away —
and the beat goes
the beat goes
the beat goes on ...

This is how I work.
This is the big magic.

The saxophone bleeds neon
and the moon sings,
the moon calls to the coyote.
I am happy happy happy happy.
I live
for jazz.

We are telling soul stories.
We are so in love
with words, with sound, with jazz.
We are so in love with the saxophone
and the red suede high-heeled shoes
and the bass.

Oh, I am drunk on jazz,
drunk on the blues,

Olive L. Sullivan

so drunk on love.
I hope —
but oh —
oh —
oh —
This is the big magic.

Salsa Mezcla

He sends me a recording of *Zueignung*,
the amethyst beaker,
the sobbing strings.

I give him Paul Simon,
Amos Lee, Joni Mitchell,
the Blackeyed Peas.

He flies me to Florence.
We tour the Uffizi,
kiss in the shadow of the Duomo,
watch fireworks from Etruscan ruins.

I take him out in my canoe
on the clear green water
that restores the mining scars —
what passes here for wilderness
and history.

He introduces my palate
to good Duero Valley wine,
truffle oil, risotto, escargot.
On Sundays we eat
fried bass sandwiches
and drink iced tea
from jelly jars.

We listen to a Willie Nelson disk
we chose together
at the Mercado in San Miguel.
When we make love,
it tastes like salsa.

Olive L. Sullivan

Pin Oak

The world is turning shades of blue,
a wall of clouds moving in from the west
to meet the darkening sky behind us.
Pin Oak Lake lies still, waiting,
a palette for the sky to fill.
Two hawks rise up, their cries
eerie in the winter dusk,
their feathers striking the last notes of gold
from the setting sun. They
wheel and circle, a dance of rage
or love or something in between —
We cannot tell. It does not matter.

Praise Song for the River

The vocabulary of praise is as varied
as the leaves breathing above us:
The very grass with its color praises Allah,
the ants toil ceaselessly toward Nirvana,
trout hang in the stream like koans,
neither question nor answer.
We come to god each in our own way
but we find ourselves on the banks of the same river,
our hot feet dangling in the same cool green water.

Olive L. Sullivan

Lake Pend Oreille

A pale piece of driftwood,
gray and gnarled, tossed
near the shore in the rocky shallows.
A rosy smooth granite stone,
wrenched from the depths
in seismic upheavals,
worn soft, the size to fit in your palm.
As the waves lap the edge of the land,
the stone and the branch
rub shoulders, nestle into
each other's curves and hollows,
shaping one to the other.

Labyrinth

Stepping, one foot in front of the other
between the stones.
Yarrow, sorrel, lamb's ear, sumac
stargrass, grass, grass, grass.
Counting the waves as they curl into the shore,
one, two, many, many, many, many.
One. One. One. One.
Learning a new way of walking.
Letting go, reading the shale and limestone,
the path of spiders, the color of driftwood,
the curl of its fingers reaching for
the mother tree.
Each twig, each leaf, each branch
an accounting of the meaning of amber.
Each number the name of a star,
each star growing green on the ground around us.
One foot stepping in front of the other.
Yarrow, sorrel, lamb's ear, sumac
stargrass, grass, grass, grass.

Olive L. Sullivan

Still

The stillness of the lake
is a gift to the dragonfly,
the bass, the mosquito,
to the small otter cutting its way
from north to south,
smoothly as a silk thread
drawn through thick green velvet,
and it's a gift to you and me,
floating together in silent communion,
the only sound the pop of your line
as it kisses the water,
is kissed in turn by
blue gill and bass.

The quarter moon's gift is
softening the too-bright light
she takes from the burning sun,
casting her reflection on the water
where my paddle dips and rises.
Her white face splashes into
half a dozen coins skipping over the surface
like smooth, flat stones,
silver ripples circling outward in their wake.

The stillness of the lake tonight
is a gift, wrapped in the
deep and varied greens of
Kansas on the cusp of summer.
Our eyes meet across the wriggling net;
we smile in secret complicity,
and I am willing you to know,
without breaking the rich green silence,
that you are a gift to me.

Tallgrass

In the straight row of junipers at Tallgrass,
I am the one leaning to the left.
I am the one watching the hawk
sitting on the farthest fence post,
the one who feels the owl's wing
brush against me like a kiss.
I am the one flying prayer flags of sky and cloud,
crimson and lavender at sunset,
rose and gold to herald the next day.
The junipers stand straight as sentinels
between the farmhouse and the grain bin.
We all reach up, stretch homeward,
but I am the one leaning to the left,
wearing songbirds in my hair.

Olive L. Sullivan

Kitchen Ballet

You slice the shallots,
set them to dancing in the skillet
while I butter your bread.
With a flick of your wrist,
you make the garlic and herbs leap
into the pan over the blue gas flame.
I pirouette left, *allongé* to
reach down cups and plates
to set the table.
We glide past each other,
our eyes meet,
our fingers *chassé* across the bread board,
and when we sit at the table,
the grand finale of our *pas de deux*,
our wine glasses clink,
our fingers brush, our eyes meet.

Everyday Mermaids

We wade hip high
through wild carrot, thick as foam,
in the center of the vanished Niobrara Sea,
a place where prehistoric monsters swam.
Now the dog leaps like a fish over waves of green.
Blackbirds skim the seedheads like gulls.

A curious bison calf,
still in its first pumpkin-colored coat,
noses a seashell, ridged and whorled
and white as bone,
fossil remnant of the ancient sea.

At the dollar store in town,
a little girl wears a tiara made in China,
her blonde hair fluorescing green in the artificial light.
She twirls and laughs
as her mother chooses a shell-shaped soap dish.

In this small town,
an island in an ocean of grass,
we're all dancing on the bottom of the long-gone sea.
From the center of the Flint Hills
we can see forever, and
forever is grass rippling in the endless south wind.

Olive L. Sullivan

Bless This House

Plant a lilac by the front porch to remember Grandma Helen,
who always liked the fragrance when she pegged out the wash.

There's no clothesline at this new house, just a high-tech LG dryer
with digital controls, complicated and expensive,
but it takes forever to dry and the clothes smell like
chemical esters, not like lilacs.

Plant iris too, the big tall ones that look like fairy castles.
Her favorites were the dark purple ones in midnight velvet.

The new house has professional landscaping,
serried ranks of hostas and small junipers
that will someday take over the porch and crack the foundation,
Japanese maples flamboyant in their burgundy silk fringe.

Plant some tulips for color in the spring.

On a night with a full moon, creep back to the old homestead
and dig up the wild honeysuckle.
Plant it by your back porch, even though your dad says he's allergic.

When your Wiccan friend brings a bundle of sage by
to smudge out unfamiliar spirits, stop her.
Hold up your hand, the one wearing Grandma's opal ring.
Say, "No. Wait."

Grab Grandma's flowered shawl.
Run out into the yard and gather arms full of honeysuckle and lilac.
Fill the whole house with their essence.
Welcome the spirits in.

Wandering Bone

About the Author

In addition to writing, Olive L. Sullivan performs in the band Amanita, and in her free time, likes to fly-fish with her husband, the scholar and writer Stephen Harmon; take long walks with dogs; and travel anywhere that requires a passport. She is an apprentice bookbinder.

Acknowledgments

To acknowledge all those who have contributed to the shaping of my poetry would take a book in itself. I'd have to list all those I've traveled with or met on the road, not to mention those who have listened as I've told stories that later became poems. A few shout-outs have to go to Mary Volenec, Pat Silovsky, Steve Harmon, and Colleen Brooks. And there is Gene DeGruson, who, as editor of The Little Balkans Review, published my very first poems, including "Avebury" (found in this collection), way back in 1982.

But I would be remiss not to mention Caryn Mirriam-Goldberg and Kelley Hunt, whose annual workshop and retreat, Brave Voice, gave me a creative community that has made all the difference. And then to thank all those who are part of that community, especially Amy Nixon, who has witnessed, shared, and helped shape my midlife reinvention.

I would also like to thank the Stonecoast MFA program at the University of Southern Maine, whose teachers and students inspired many of the poems in this volume, especially Jeanne Marie Beaumont, Breena Clarke, and Debra Marquart, who pushed me to go "wilder and deeper" and to question everything I thought I knew about writing and about life.

And of course I'd like to thank my family, especially my sons Frank and Jacob Abshire, who were dragged to several early poetry readings and lived through many of the events that appear, transformed, hopefully for the better, in this book. I'd also like to thank my daughter-in-law, Angel Abshire. If I'd known how cool daughters-in-law could be, I'd have had them first.

Olive L. Sullivan

Credits

"Everyday Mermaids," *Konza: A Bioregional Journal on Living in Place,* The Kansas Area Watershed Council, Lawrence, Kan.: Fall 2017.

"Bless This House," *Konza: A Bioregional Journal on Living in Place,* The Kansas Area Watershed Council, Lawrence, Kan.: Fall 2017.

"Pin Oak," *Konza: A Bioregional Journal on Living in Place,* The Kansas Area Watershed Council, Lawrence, Kan.: Fall 2017.

"Pin Oak," *Where I Live Poetry and Photography Series,* Silver Birch Press, March 17, 2015.

"Smiley's Bar," *Midwest Quarterly,* Summer 2014.

"The Bone Goddess," *Mythic Poetry Series,* Silver Birch Press, Oct. 7, 2014.

"Driving West," *Begin Again: 150 Kansas Poems,* ed. Caryn Mirriam-Goldberg. Woodley Press, Topeka, Kan.: 2011.

"The Seventh Year," *Begin Again: 150 Kansas Poems,* ed. Caryn Mirriam-Goldberg. Woodley Press, Topeka, Kan.: 2011.

"Labyrinth," as "Grass," York Unitarians newsletter, York, England: Sept./Oct. 2007.

"Landslip," *Radiance: The Magazine for Large Women,* Oakland, Calif.: Spring 1997.

"Coming Back from New Mexico at Night," *Puma Prints,* the newsletter of the Chihuahuan Desert Conservation Alliance, Carlsbad, NM: April 1995.

"Gas Station Guru," *Resonance: One World, Many Voices,* Summer 1994.

"Avebury," *The Little Balkans Review,* Pittsburg, Kan.: Fall/Winter 1982.

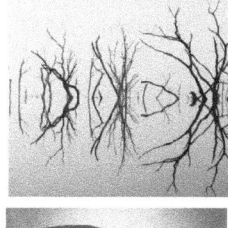
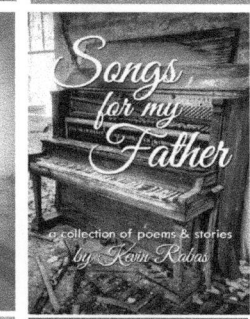

WWW.MEADOWLARK-BOOKS.COM

Specializing in Books by Authors from the Heartland since 2014

www.ingramcontent.com/pod-product-compliance
Lightning Source LLC
Chambersburg PA
CBHW020945090426
42736CB00010B/1270